Digital Random Art:
Exploring Infinite Possibilities in Creativity

With Additional Random Art Ornaments

Edmond Carlson

CONTENTS

Chapter   Pg.

Chapter   Pg.

Chapter	Pg.

Introduction to Digital Random Art

Welcome to the world of Digital Random Art, a captivating journey into the realm of artistic expression driven by randomness. This innovative form of creative exploration utilizes the power of random number generators to craft an endless array of unique artworks and designs. Whether you're an experienced artist or someone with minimal artistic skills, this e-Book will introduce you to the exciting world of Digital Random Art and show you how to unlock your creativity in ways you never thought possible.

Conclusion: Embrace the Unexpected Beauty

As you embark on this voyage through the world of Digital Random Art, remember that every stroke of randomness has the potential to unveil a masterpiece. Whether you're seeking a new form of artistic expression, a creative outlet, or a way to enhance your design skills, Digital Random Art offers a doorway to limitless inspiration and innovation. Embrace the beauty of the unexpected and let your imagination run wild as you immerse yourself in the captivating universe of Digital Random Art.

1. Understanding Digital Random Art

In this chapter, we'll delve into the core concepts that define Digital Random Art and explore how randomness breathes life into artistic creations.

Defining Digital Random Art

Digital Random Art is a fascinating genre that combines the serendipitous nature of randomness with the creative expressions of art. Unlike traditional art forms where the artist's intentions guide every stroke, Digital Random Art introduces an element of chance through the use of random number generators. This convergence of technology and art opens up new avenues for creativity, enabling artists to co-create with the unknown and bring forth unexpected beauty.

The Role of Randomness in Art

Randomness has a profound impact on the creative process, often leading to outcomes that surprise even the artist. In traditional art, every decision is deliberate, calculated, and meticulously executed. However, Digital Random Art challenges this paradigm by introducing randomness as an active participant in the creative journey. By relinquishing some control and allowing chance to guide certain aspects of the artwork, artists tap into the infinite realm of possibilities, resulting in pieces that possess a unique, organic allure.

How Random Number Generators Work

At the heart of Digital Random Art lies the random number generator (RNG), a computational tool that produces sequences of numbers without any predictable pattern. These generators are governed by complex algorithms that leverage factors such as time, user input, and system variables to generate seemingly arbitrary values. When applied to art, RNGs determine various elements like line placement, color selection, and pattern formation. By harnessing the power of RNGs, artists introduce an element of surprise into their creative process, sparking new ideas and pushing the boundaries of conventional artistry.

In the next chapter, we'll guide you through the process of getting started with Digital Random Art, providing you with essential tools and insights to embark on your creative journey.

2. Getting Started with Digital Random Art

In this chapter, we'll equip you with the fundamental knowledge and tools you need to embark on your Digital Random Art journey. From essential software to crafting your creative space, you'll be well-prepared to explore the endless possibilities of this innovative art form.

Essential Tools and Software

Before diving into the world of Digital Random Art, it's essential to have the right tools at your disposal. You'll need a computer or tablet with basic hardware specifications to run the necessary software smoothly. Additionally, you'll require graphic design software that supports randomization features, allowing you to harness the power of random number generators to create your artworks. We'll explore some popular software options and guide you on how to choose the one that suits your needs best.

Setting Up Your Workspace

Creating Digital Random Art requires a dedicated workspace that fosters creativity and concentration. Whether it's a cozy corner of your room or a fully-equipped studio, your workspace should be free from distractions and conducive to artistic exploration. We'll share tips on organizing your tools, optimizing lighting conditions, and arranging your workstation to maximize your creative potential.

Basic Concepts and Techniques

As you embark on your Digital Random Art journey, it's essential to grasp some foundational concepts and techniques that will serve as your artistic compass. We'll introduce you to concepts like line generation, shape manipulation, color randomization, and pattern formation. You'll learn how to wield these elements using random number generators to create compelling compositions that transcend traditional artistic boundaries. Through step-by-step explanations and illustrative examples, we'll empower you to experiment with these techniques and infuse your artworks with a touch of randomness.

In the next chapter, we'll dive deeper into the creative process of Digital Random Art, exploring different styles and approaches that will spark your imagination and push your artistic boundaries.

3. Creating Your First Digital Random Artwork

Now that you have a solid grasp of the foundational concepts, it's time to roll up your sleeves and create your very first Digital Random Artwork. In this chapter, we'll guide you through the process of generating your artwork from scratch, using various techniques and tools to infuse randomness into your creations.

Exploring Line Generation

Lines are the building blocks of art, and in Digital Random Art, they become dynamic and unpredictable. We'll introduce you to the concept of line generation, where you'll harness the power of random number generators to create intricate and unpredictable line patterns. You'll learn how to control factors such as length, angle, and thickness, allowing you to produce an array of captivating line compositions. Through hands-on exercises and practical tips, you'll see how these random lines can form the foundation of unique and mesmerizing artworks.

Unleashing Your Imagination with Shapes

Shapes are the canvas upon which your creativity takes form. We'll delve into the world of shape manipulation, where you'll learn how to use randomization to create a multitude of shapes, from simple polygons to intricate designs. You'll explore techniques to adjust parameters like size, rotation, and position, enabling you to produce an endless array of shape variations. By embracing randomness, you'll break free from conventional artistic constraints and unlock your imagination to craft artworks that are truly one-of-a-kind.

Playing with Colors and Patterns

Color and pattern add depth and vibrancy to your creations, and in

Digital Random Art, they're yours to command. We'll show you how to experiment with color palettes and patterns by employing randomization techniques. Discover how random number generators can guide your color choices, allowing you to explore harmonious and unexpected color combinations. Moreover, you'll learn how to create mesmerizing patterns by blending randomness with symmetry, resulting in captivating artworks that engage the eye and evoke emotions.

With these skills under your belt, you're ready to embark on a creative journey that's as exciting as it is unpredictable. In the next chapter, we'll explore advanced techniques and methods that will push your Digital Random Art to new heights, enabling you to craft artworks that transcend imagination.

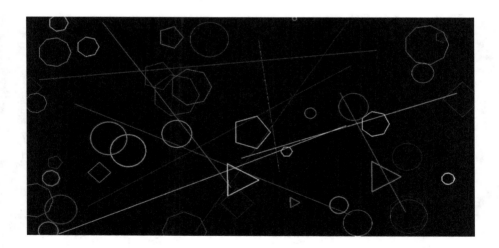

4. Diving Deeper: Advanced Techniques

In this chapter, we'll take your Digital Random Art to the next level by delving into advanced techniques that will elevate your creations from intriguing to extraordinary. As you become more comfortable with the basics, it's time to explore new horizons and push the boundaries of what's possible.

Layering and Composition

Just like a painter applies layers of paint to a canvas, you'll learn how to layer elements in your Digital Random Art to create depth and complexity. By combining different layers with distinct patterns, colors, and shapes, you'll achieve stunning compositions that draw viewers in and captivate their imagination.

Textures and Effects

Textures and effects add tactile qualities to your digital creations, transforming them into multi-dimensional experiences. We'll show you how to introduce textures through the power of randomness. Additionally, you'll explore effects, allowing you to manipulate your artwork's visual appearance in innovative and compelling ways. By embracing these techniques, you'll bring a new level of richness and intrigue to your Digital Random Art.

Incorporating User Input

Art is a dialogue between the creator and the viewer, and incorporating user input can transform your Digital Random Art into an interactive experience. Discover how to integrate user-defined parameters and interactions into your creations, allowing viewers to influence the outcome of your artworks. Whether it's adjusting colors, altering patterns, or even determining the overall composition, you'll empower your audience to become part of the artistic process. This engagement adds a dynamic and participatory dimension to your art, fostering a deeper connection between your creations and their observers.

By embracing these advanced techniques, you'll have the tools to craft artworks that astonish and inspire. The tenth chapter of this book will guide you through the process of sharing your Digital Random Art with the world, exploring platforms, exhibitions, and communities that celebrate and showcase innovative digital creations.

5. Incorporating Digital Random Art in Design

As we expand our horizons beyond traditional art, we delve into the exciting realm of design. Digital Random Art isn't limited to just being visually captivating; it can also serve as a powerful tool for design professionals seeking new ways to innovate and communicate.

Design Prototyping and Ideation

Designers constantly seek fresh perspectives to fuel their creativity, and Digital Random Art offers a unique avenue for ideation. Learn how to harness randomness to generate design concepts and prototypes that break away from the expected. By infusing your design process with unexpected elements, you'll unlock novel ideas that have the potential to transform industries and redefine aesthetics.

Applying Random Art in User Interfaces

User interfaces (UI) play a pivotal role in modern design, shaping how users interact with technology. Discover how to integrate Digital Random Art principles into UI design to craft interfaces that are not only functional but also visually engaging. By strategically incorporating random patterns, colors, and shapes, you'll create interfaces that resonate with users on a deeper level, enhancing their digital experiences.

Enhancing Visual Communication

Communication is at the heart of design, and Digital Random Art provides a fresh language for expressing ideas. Explore how to leverage randomness to convey emotions, concepts, and messages in your designs. Whether you're designing logos, posters, or digital illustrations, these techniques will help you infuse your work with an organic and dynamic quality, making your visual communication more impactful and memorable.

By embracing Digital Random Art in the world of design, you'll forge a bridge between creativity and functionality, sparking innovation and captivating audiences. As you embark on this journey, consider the ethical implications of using randomness as a design tool and explore ways to strike a balance between creative chaos and purposeful design. In the eleventh chapter, we'll reflect on the ecological and economical advantages of Digital Random Art, underscoring its sustainability and potential for positive change.

6. Utilizing Digital Random Art in Education

Education is a realm where creativity and innovation hold immense value. Incorporating Digital Random Art into educational settings opens up a world of possibilities, enriching the learning experience and nurturing creative thinking in students of all ages.

Fostering Creativity in Children

Children possess innate curiosity and boundless imagination, making them ideal candidates for exploring the wonders of Digital Random Art. Discover how educators can introduce this innovative approach in classrooms to foster creativity. By encouraging students to interact with randomness, they'll develop the capacity to think outside the box, envision novel solutions, and embrace the unexpected—a skill set that will serve them well in various aspects of life.

Teaching Concepts through Art

Art has the remarkable ability to convey complex concepts in a visually appealing manner. Explore how educators can leverage Digital Random Art to teach subjects across the curriculum. Whether it's mathematics, science, history, or literature, creating artworks infused with random elements can provide students with a unique perspective that enhances their understanding of abstract ideas and encourages critical thinking.

Interactive Learning Experiences

Digital Random Art transcends traditional teaching methods by offering interactive and immersive learning experiences. Delve into ways educators can integrate hands-on activities involving Digital Random Art to engage students on a deeper level. From collaborative art projects that encourage teamwork to interactive software that lets students generate their own art, these experiences can transform learning into an exciting adventure that empowers students to explore, experiment, and express themselves freely.

As we witness the transformative potential of Digital Random Art in education, it's crucial to address its ethical dimensions. Engage in discussions with students about the balance between randomness and intention in art, fostering an appreciation for both controlled design and unanticipated beauty. As we wrap up our exploration, we'll celebrate the ecologically and economically conscious nature of Digital Random Art, illustrating how it aligns with modern sensibilities and the quest for sustainable creativity.

7. Exploring Different Styles and Genres

One of the captivating aspects of Digital Random Art is its ability to span a wide spectrum of styles and genres, allowing artists to venture into uncharted territories and create artworks that resonate with diverse aesthetics. In this section, we'll delve into three distinct styles that thrive when infused with randomness, resulting in breathtaking creations that captivate the senses and stir the imagination.

Abstract Random Art

The realm of abstract art embraces the unexpected and the intangible. Discover how Digital Random Art offers a natural ally to abstract expressionism, enabling artists to channel raw emotions and spontaneous gestures. We'll explore techniques for generating abstract compositions that evoke a wide range of feelings and interpretations, showcasing how the convergence of chance and intention can lead to mesmerizing visual narratives.

Geometric Patterns and Symmetry

Geometric art finds harmony in precision, symmetry, and mathematical forms. Journey through the realm of Digital Random Art as it collaborates with geometry, transcending ordered repetition to embrace the unpredictable. Learn how to create intricate patterns that balance structure and randomness, resulting in captivating designs that offer a new perspective on the marriage between mathematical elegance and artistic freedom.

Landscape and Nature-Inspired Art

Nature has long been an inspiration for artists, evoking feelings of tranquility, wonder, and awe. Discover how Digital Random Art can be a conduit for nature's unpredictable beauty, allowing artists to channel the essence of landscapes onto digital canvases. Whether it's recreating the textures of natural elements or capturing the ebb and flow of organic forms, this exploration into nature-inspired randomness will unveil the breathtaking potential of creative synergy.

As we traverse these diverse styles and genres, you'll uncover the versatility of Digital Random Art and its capacity to bridge the gap between artistic traditions and contemporary innovation. Each style presents a unique playground for experimentation, where the unexpected becomes a cherished collaborator in the creative process. Join us as we traverse the landscapes of abstraction, geometry, and nature-inspired art, unearthing the profound possibilities that arise when randomness dances with intention on the digital canvas.

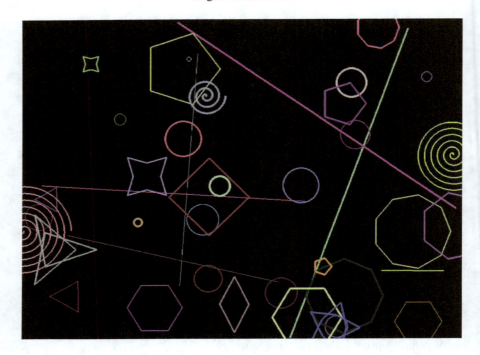

8. The Impact of Digital Random Art

In this era of rapid technological evolution, Digital Random Art emerges as a testament to the boundless potential that lies at the intersection of art and technology. Its influence reverberates far beyond the realm of creative expression, touching various facets of contemporary culture and fostering new dialogues between artists, audiences, and the digital world. Join us as we explore the profound impact of Digital Random Art on the creative landscape, from reshaping artistic paradigms to spotlighting the innovators who have harnessed its power.

Shaping the Future of Digital Creativity

Digital Random Art is at the forefront of a creative revolution, redefining the way we perceive, create, and engage with visual art. This chapter delves into the transformative influence that randomness injects into the creative process, fostering innovation and pushing the boundaries of artistic experimentation. From generative algorithms to interactive installations, the future of digital creativity is being written with each stroke of the random art brush.

Artist Spotlights: Random Art in the Contemporary Art Scene

Embark on a journey through the contemporary art scene, where Digital Random Art has found its voice among a new generation of creators. We shine a spotlight on artists who have harnessed the power of randomness to craft captivating visual narratives that captivate audiences and challenge artistic conventions. Through their stories, you'll witness how Digital Random Art has become a vessel for personal expression, societal commentary, and a fresh take on traditional mediums.

Art and Technology: A Symbiotic Relationship

As technology evolves, so too does the artistic landscape. In this exploration, we investigate the symbiotic relationship between art and technology, tracing their intertwined evolution and the ways in which Digital Random Art stands as a beacon of innovation. From the democratization of artistic tools to the fusion of traditional techniques with digital mediums, you'll gain insights into how technology's embrace has enriched and expanded the horizons of the artistic realm.

Join us as we navigate the impact of Digital Random Art, transcending traditional definitions of art and ushering in a new era of creative expression. As we peer into the future, it becomes evident that the dynamic synergy between randomness and digital tools holds the key to unlocking artistic potential yet to be imagined.

9. Practical Tips for Creating Stunning Random Art

Crafting captivating Digital Random Art goes beyond understanding the technicalities; it's about embracing the inherent unpredictability and harnessing it to your advantage. In this chapter, we offer invaluable tips that will elevate your random art creations from intriguing to truly exceptional. Discover how to find inspiration in the midst of unpredictability, strike the perfect balance between intuition and technique, and embrace the imperfections that lend your creations their distinctive charm.

Finding Inspiration in Unpredictability

The essence of Digital Random Art lies in its very unpredictability. As you embark on your creative journey, open yourself to the beauty of the unknown. Let randomness guide you towards uncharted territories, and don't shy away from the unexpected outcomes that may arise. These unforeseen elements often become the sparks that ignite your imagination and breathe life into your artwork, leading you down avenues you might never have ventured otherwise.

Combining Intuition and Technique

While randomness plays a central role, your intuition and artistic sensibilities remain indispensable. Explore the symbiotic relationship between intuition and technique, allowing them to coalesce in harmonious synergy. Direct your instincts to guide the creative process, while your technical prowess channels those instincts into visually striking compositions. This balance ensures that your random art is not just a product of chance, but a deliberate manifestation of your artistic vision.

Embracing Imperfections for Unique Beauty

Imperfections in art often carry the allure of authenticity. In the realm of Digital Random Art, these imperfections become touchstones of uniqueness and character. Embrace the quirks and irregularities that may emerge from the randomness, for they bestow your creations with a distinct charm that sets them apart. Remember, it's not about achieving pixel-perfect precision; it's about embracing the individuality that arises from the dance between your creative intentions and the random elements.

As you apply these practical tips to your Digital Random Art endeavors, you'll find yourself navigating the fine line between control and chaos, resulting in creations that are not only visually stunning but also rich with the stories of their creation. Embrace the journey, and let the unpredictable nature of randomness be your guide to unlocking unparalleled artistic heights.

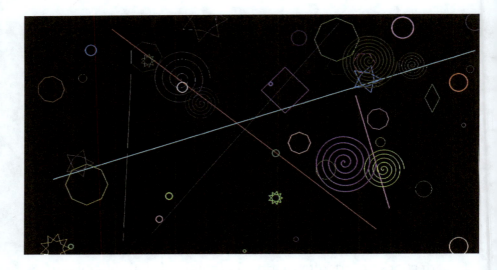

10. Sharing and Showcasing Your Digital Random Art

Your journey through the realm of Digital Random Art is an exploration of creativity, unpredictability, and boundless possibilities. As you create captivating pieces of art, you'll inevitably want to share your creations with the world. This chapter delves into the exciting realm of sharing and showcasing your Digital Random Art, from connecting with online communities to building a compelling portfolio and engaging with audiences and collectors.

Online Platforms and Communities

In the digital age, the internet offers an array of platforms and communities eager to embrace your Digital Random Art. Social media platforms, art-sharing websites, and specialized online forums provide spaces where you can display your creations, receive feedback, and connect with fellow artists and enthusiasts. These platforms not only showcase your work but also offer opportunities for collaboration, inspiration, and growth within a global artistic community.

Building Your Random Art Portfolio

A well-curated portfolio is a testament to your artistic journey and growth. Organize your Digital Random Art into a coherent collection that reflects your evolution as an artist. A portfolio showcases the diverse range of styles, techniques, and themes you've explored, capturing the essence of your creative identity. Whether in physical or digital form, your portfolio serves as a compelling visual narrative that invites viewers to delve into your world of randomness and artistry.

Engaging with Audiences and Collectors

The journey of an artist is enriched by the conversations and connections formed with audiences and collectors. Engage with those who appreciate your work by sharing insights into your creative process, the stories behind your pieces, and the significance of randomness in your art. Cultivate relationships with collectors who are drawn to the unique allure of your Digital Random Art. The dynamic between artist and audience adds depth to the experience of your art and can lead to collaborations, exhibitions, and even commercial success.

As you step into the realm of sharing and showcasing, remember that each interaction is an opportunity to inspire, spark conversations, and create a lasting impact. Embrace the power of digital connectivity to extend your creative reach and share the magic of Digital Random Art with a global audience eager to immerse themselves in the beauty of chance and creativity.

11. Eco-Friendly and Economical Aspects of Digital Random Art

Beyond the realm of artistic creation, Digital Random Art offers an unexpected advantage that resonates with both environmental consciousness and economic sensibility. This chapter delves into the eco-friendly and economical aspects of Digital Random Art, highlighting its potential to minimize environmental impact, provide low-cost creative endeavors, and champion a sustainable approach to artistic expression.

Minimizing Environmental Impact

In a world that increasingly values sustainability, Digital Random Art emerges as a responsible choice for artists. Unlike traditional art forms that consume paper, canvases, pigments, and other materials,

Digital Random Art requires no physical resources. By harnessing the power of digital tools, artists can create endlessly without depleting natural resources or contributing to waste. This eco-conscious approach aligns with the ethos of reducing one's carbon footprint and safeguarding the environment for future generations.

Low-Cost Creative Endeavors

Artistic expression should be accessible to all, and Digital Random Art upholds this principle through its low-cost nature. While traditional art forms often require investment in supplies and equipment, Digital Random Art requires only a digital device and suitable software. This affordability democratizes art creation, enabling individuals from diverse backgrounds to explore their creativity without financial barriers. Whether you're a seasoned artist or a novice, Digital Random Art invites you to embark on a journey of self-expression without the burden of exorbitant costs.

A Sustainable Approach to Artistic Expression

Artists wield a unique influence in shaping cultural perspectives, and with that influence comes the responsibility to inspire positive change. Digital Random Art pioneers a sustainable approach to artistic expression, encouraging artists to explore new dimensions while safeguarding the planet. By adopting digital platforms, artists contribute to a movement that reimagines creativity as a force for good—a force that respects nature, promotes accessibility, and aligns with the global call for sustainable practices.

As you embark on your Digital Random Art journey, remember that your creative endeavors have the power to make a difference beyond the canvas. By choosing a sustainable and economical approach to art, you become part of a movement that honors creativity, supports the environment, and promotes artistic inclusivity on a global scale.

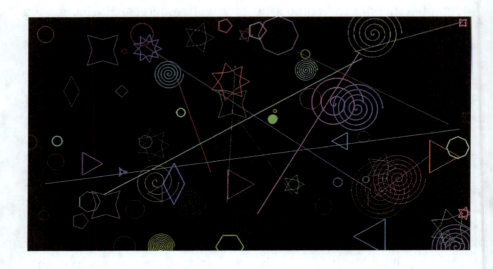

12. Troubleshooting and Overcoming Challenges

The path of a digital artist, even within the realm of Digital Random Art, is not devoid of challenges. In this chapter, we delve into strategies for troubleshooting and overcoming obstacles, ensuring that your artistic journey remains a smooth and fulfilling one. From creative blocks to technical glitches, we address the most common challenges that artists encounter and provide guidance to help you navigate through them.

Dealing with Creative Blocks

Creative blocks are a universal experience, even for the most seasoned artists. When inspiration feels elusive and your creative well runs dry, it's important to remember that these moments are part of the creative process. Embrace them as opportunities for introspection and growth. Engage in activities that inspire you, take a break to clear your mind, and explore new subjects or techniques.

Sometimes, stepping away from your work and returning with fresh eyes can rekindle your creative spark.

Technical Issues and Solutions

The digital realm comes with its fair share of technical challenges, from software glitches to hardware malfunctions. In the world of Digital Random Art, these challenges can range from unexpected errors in algorithms to software crashes. When faced with technical issues, remain patient and methodical. Start by saving your progress regularly and utilizing version control. Keep your software and hardware up to date, and don't hesitate to seek help from online communities, forums, or customer support. Remember, technical difficulties are surmountable, and each hurdle you overcome strengthens your artistic resilience.

Navigating Common Artistic Dilemmas

Artistic dilemmas often stem from questions of style, composition, and intent. When creating Digital Random Art, you might encounter dilemmas related to color choices, pattern placements, or the overall coherence of your artwork. In such moments, it's helpful to step back and evaluate your work from a broader perspective. Seek feedback from peers, mentors, or art communities to gain fresh insights. Don't be afraid to experiment and explore different approaches; after all, the essence of Digital Random Art lies in embracing the unexpected.

As you navigate through challenges, both creative and technical, remember that every obstacle you overcome contributes to your growth as an artist. Approach setbacks with patience and a problem-solving mindset, and view them as opportunities to refine your skills and deepen your understanding of Digital Random Art. Just as your art evolves, so too does your ability to adapt and thrive in the face of challenges.

13. Random Art Collaborations and Projects

In the interconnected digital landscape, collaboration has taken on new dimensions, enabling artists to transcend geographical boundaries and create together in ways previously unimaginable. In this chapter, we explore the realm of Random Art collaborations and projects, shedding light on the power of collective creativity, the formation of art collectives and communities, and the exciting opportunities for collective creations and exhibitions.

Collaborative Art in the Digital Age

The digital age has redefined collaboration, allowing artists from diverse backgrounds to collaborate seamlessly on a single canvas. Collaborative Random Art projects exemplify the fusion of artistic visions and voices, resulting in captivating visual narratives that transcend individual perspectives. Through online platforms and tools, artists can contribute their unique elements to a shared artwork, weaving together a tapestry of creativity that captures the essence of collective expression.

Generating Art Collectives and Communities

Art collectives and communities are vibrant hubs that bring together artists who share common interests, styles, or goals. These virtual spaces foster collaboration, networking, and the exchange of ideas, serving as incubators for innovation. Within these collectives, Random Art serves as a dynamic medium that promotes experimentation, pushing the boundaries of artistic creation. By joining or forming art collectives, artists can tap into a wellspring of support, inspiration, and shared artistic growth.

Collective Creations and Exhibition Opportunities

Collective Random Art creations are more than the sum of their individual parts; they are collaborative journeys that showcase the power of artistic unity. These creations can be unveiled through online galleries, social media platforms, or curated exhibitions. Such exhibitions highlight the diversity of artistic perspectives while celebrating the collaborative spirit. In an era where physical and virtual boundaries blur, Random Art collectives and projects create bridges between artists, viewers, and the digital canvas.

Whether you're collaborating on an international project or participating in a community-driven endeavor, Random Art collaborations foster connections that transcend distances and unite creative energies. Embrace the richness of collaborative creation, and explore the boundless possibilities of Random Art within collective projects. Through these collaborations, you not only amplify your artistic voice but also contribute to a global tapestry of creative expression.

14. Legal and Copyright Considerations

As you journey through the world of Random Art and digital creativity, it's essential to be aware of the legal and copyright considerations that come into play. Protecting your artistic creations, understanding copyright and licensing, and navigating the intricate landscape of intellectual property are crucial steps to ensure your work is respected and used appropriately.

Protecting Your Random Art Creations

Your Random Art creations are a product of your creativity, time, and effort. To safeguard your artistic endeavors, consider strategies such as watermarking your work, using digital signatures, and adding metadata to your files. These steps can help deter unauthorized use and provide a trail of ownership in case of disputes.

Understanding Copyright and Licensing

Copyright is the legal framework that grants creators exclusive rights to their original works. While copyright is automatically assigned to you upon creating a piece of Random Art, understanding the scope of your rights and how they can be legally enforced is paramount. Additionally, licensing options allow you to grant specific permissions for others to use your work under certain conditions, enabling you to retain control over how your creations are shared and utilized.

Navigating Intellectual Property in Digital Art

In the digital realm, issues related to intellectual property can be complex. It's essential to respect the intellectual property rights of others and obtain proper permissions when incorporating elements from third-party sources. When collaborating on Random Art projects, clearly define ownership and usage rights to avoid conflicts down the line. Keep thorough records of your work's development process, as these can be invaluable in demonstrating your original authorship.

As you explore the exciting possibilities of Random Art, remember that your creations hold artistic and legal value. By staying informed about legal considerations, copyright laws, and intellectual property rights, you empower yourself to protect your work and make informed decisions about how it's shared and used. Through responsible stewardship of your Random Art, you contribute to the preservation and respect of digital creativity across the global artistic community.

15. Future Trends and Innovations in Digital Random Art

The realm of Digital Random Art is a dynamic and ever-evolving landscape, constantly shaped by technological advancements, creative exploration, and the ever-expanding boundaries of human imagination. As you delve deeper into this creative medium, it's fascinating to consider the future trends and innovations that will further redefine the possibilities of Random Art.

AI and Machine Learning in Random Art

Artificial Intelligence (AI) and Machine Learning (ML) are poised to play an increasingly significant role in the world of Random Art. Imagine algorithms that not only generate shapes and colors but also learn from your artistic preferences, leading to more personalized and intuitive creative processes. AI-driven tools may even assist in the selection of elements, colors, and patterns, providing a harmonious collaboration between human creativity and computational intelligence.

Interactive and Immersive Random Art Experiences

The boundaries between art and technology continue to blur, giving rise to interactive and immersive Random Art experiences. Augmented Reality (AR) and Virtual Reality (VR) platforms offer new dimensions for displaying your Random Art creations, allowing viewers to engage with and experience your work in unprecedented ways. Imagine users stepping into your digital realm, surrounded by swirling colors and shapes that respond to their every movement.

The Evolving Landscape of Artistic Expression

Random Art is at the forefront of redefining artistic expression in the digital age. The ongoing fusion of technology and creativity challenges traditional notions of artistry, inviting artists to embrace unpredictability and experimentation in their work. As society becomes increasingly digital, Random Art stands as a testament to the limitless potential of human innovation, and its continued evolution will undoubtedly shape the future of art and creativity.

By embracing these future trends and innovations, you position yourself at the forefront of the Digital Random Art movement. As you experiment with AI-driven tools, create interactive experiences, and explore new mediums, you contribute to the ongoing transformation of how art is created, shared, and experienced. The canvas of the digital world is vast, and your Random Artistry has the power to illuminate new paths for artistic expression in the years to come.

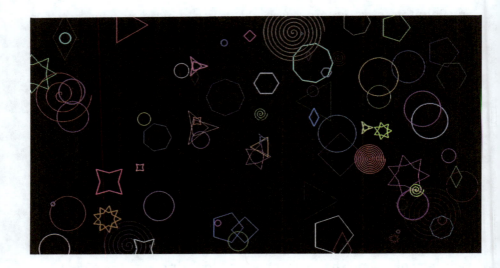

16. Your Journey Continues: Experimentation and Exploration

As you conclude your immersive exploration of the world of Digital Random Art, remember that your creative journey is far from over. In fact, this is just the beginning—a launchpad into a world of endless experimentation, boundary-pushing, and creative growth.

Pushing the Boundaries of Random Art

Now armed with a wealth of knowledge and techniques, it's time to challenge the very essence of Random Art. Push its boundaries, bend its rules, and stretch your imagination to new horizons. Combine unexpected elements, merge various styles, and let your creativity flow freely. Through this fearless exploration, you have the power to redefine the art form itself, forging a new path that is uniquely yours.

Mixing Media and Techniques

While Digital Random Art thrives in the digital realm, don't be afraid to mix media and techniques. Integrate traditional art forms, experiment with physical materials, or combine your digital creations with tangible objects. The fusion of different artistic mediums can lead to astonishing results that transcend the confines of any single medium.

Cultivating a Lifelong Creative Adventure

Remember, your journey as a Digital Random Artist is a lifelong adventure—one that evolves alongside your growth as an artist and a person. Embrace the fluidity of creativity and the evolving nature of technology. Seek inspiration from the world around you, engage in diverse artistic endeavors, and remain open to unexpected twists and turns. The beauty of this journey lies in its unpredictability and the vast opportunities it presents.

As you embark on the next chapter of your creative voyage, carry with you the spirit of exploration, curiosity, and the boundless joy of creating something truly unique. Your palette is the universe itself, and your canvas knows no limits. So, go forth with confidence, continue to experiment, and let the world of Digital Random Art be your endless playground of innovation and expression.

17. Links

21 web links that you might find valuable for exploring and diving deeper into the world of Digital Random Art:

1. **Random Art on Facebook**: Follow to **Random Art**: facebook.com/61550313433710

2. **eTestinf**: Subscribe to YouTube channel about Python coding and Random Art Generators: youtube.com/channel/UC7-4VoA_SKAxNxktDySof-Q

3. **Generative Artistry**: An educational platform with tutorials, resources, and articles on generative art and coding: generativeartistry.com

4. **Creative Applications**: A platform that showcases the

intersection of art, design, and technology, featuring various generative and digital art projects: creativeapplications.net

5. **Processing Foundation**: A programming language and environment for creative coding, ideal for creating digital art and generative designs: processingfoundation.org

6. **OpenProcessing**: An online community platform for sharing, exploring, and discussing generative art created with the Processing language: openprocessing.org

7. **ArtStation**: A platform to discover and showcase digital art from artists around the world, including generative and random art pieces: artstation.com

8. **Behance**: Explore a diverse range of digital art projects and portfolios, including generative and algorithmic art: behance.net

9. **Tumblr - Generative Art**: A tag-specific search for generative art on Tumblr, featuring a wide variety of works from different artists: tumblr.com/tagged/generative-art/

10. **Reddit - Generative Art**: A Reddit community dedicated to generative art discussions, sharing projects, and learning resources: reddit.com/r/generative/

11. **AI Art Generator**: An AI-powered art generator that creates unique and surreal art pieces using neural networks: deepdreamgenerator.com

12. **Interactive, Digital Art Museum in Tokyo**: MORI Building DIGITAL ART MUSEUM, Tokyo: teamlab.art/e/borderless_azabudai

13. **Rhizome**: Stories of Rhizome and Generative Art: rhizome.org/editorial/2023/jul/28/seed-stories-of-rhizome-and-generative-art

14. **Random.org**: A true random number generator and randomization service that can be used for generating random elements in your artwork: random.org

15. **The Coding Train**: A YouTube channel with tutorials, challenges, and explorations in creative coding, including generative art projects: thecodingtrain.com

16. **Generative Hut**: A blog and resource hub for generative art enthusiasts, offering tutorials, tools, and inspiration: generativehut.com

17. **Digital Art Museum**: An online collection of digital art, including generative and algorithmic creations: digitalartmuseum.org

18. **Artificial Intelligence Art**: A community-driven platform showcasing artwork created with the help of artificial intelligence and algorithms: aiartists.org

19. **Processing Community Day**: An annual event celebrating creative coding and generative art within the Processing community: processingfoundation.org

20. **Generative Art**: Generative art in Wikipedia: en.wikipedia.org/wiki/Generative_art

21. **OpenAI:** OpenAI is an AI research and deployment company: openai.com

These links cover a wide range of topics, from coding resources and online platforms to inspirational galleries and AI-driven art generators. They can help you further explore the fascinating world of Digital Random Art and deepen your understanding of its various aspects.

Follow to Random Art: facebook.com/61550313433710

Edmond Carlson

Sept., 2023

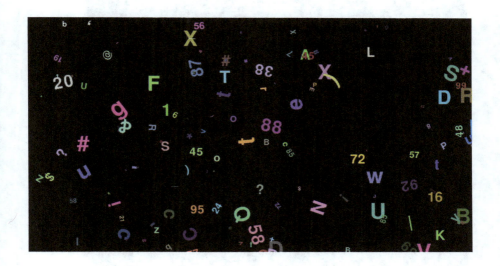

18. Additional Random Art Ornaments

1. Random lines

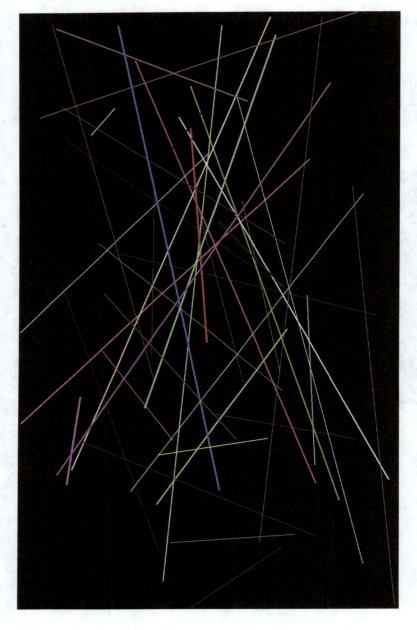

2. Random circles

3. Random rectangles

4. Random rectangles and stars

5. Random spirals

6. Random lines and circles

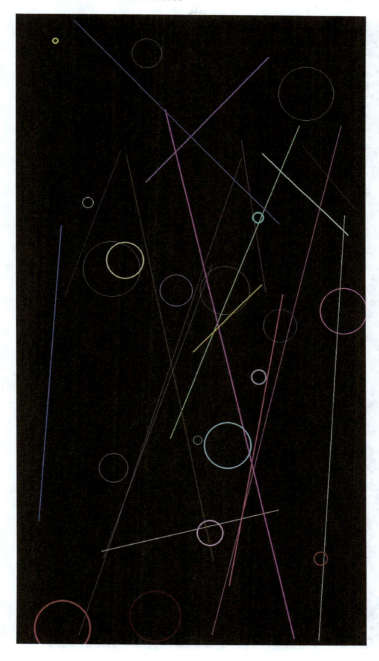

7. Random lines and rectangles

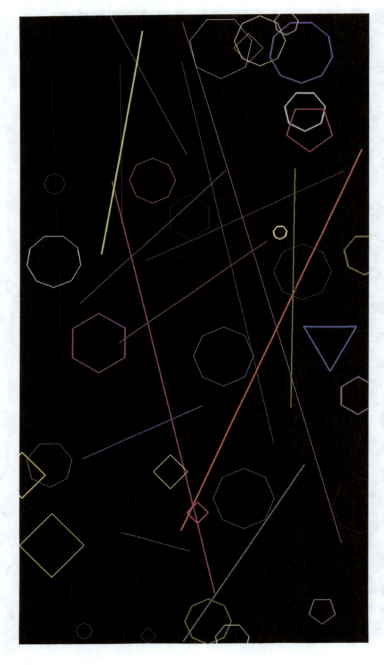

8.   Random lines, rectangles and stars.

9. Random lines and spirals

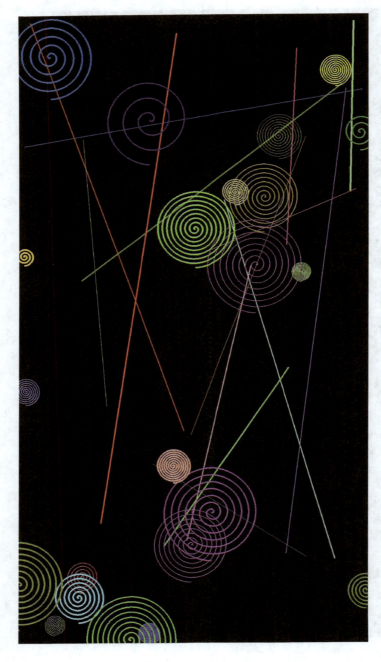

10. Random lines, circles and rectangles

11. Random lines, rectangles and stars

12. Random lines, circles and spirals

13. Random lines, circles, rectangles and stars

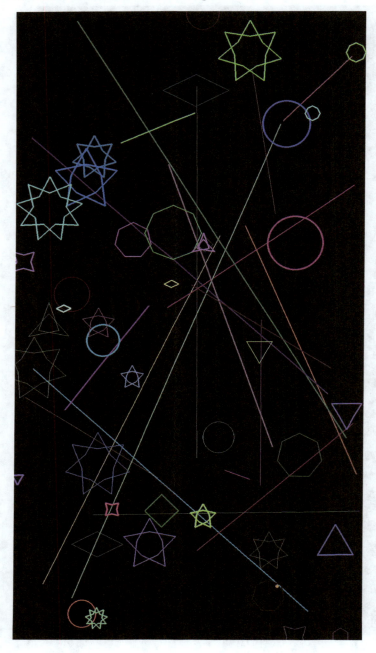

14. Random lines, circles and rectangles

15. Random lines, rectangles and spirals

16. Random lines, rectangles and stars

17. Random lines, circles, rectangles, stars and spirals

18. Random lines, circles, rectangles, stars, spirals and bacground color.

19. Random ornament with colorful rectangles

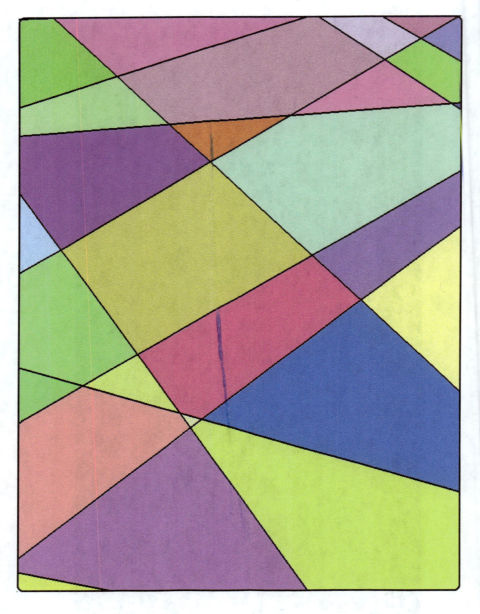

20. Random ornament with colorful rectangles

21. Random ornament with colorful rectangles

22. Random ornament with colorful rectangles

23. Random ornament with colorful rectangles

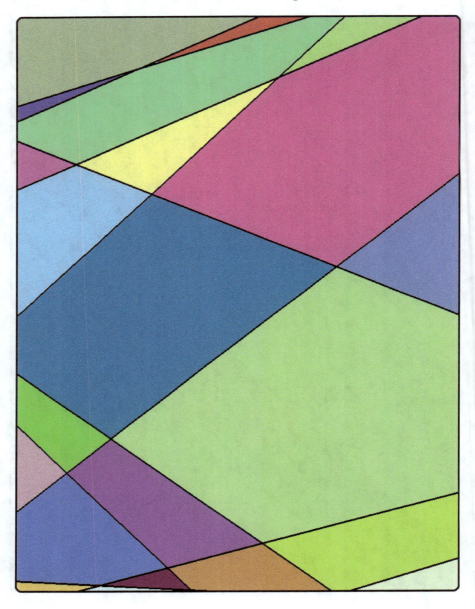

24. Random ornament with colorful rectangles

25. Random ornament with colorful rectangles

26. Random ornament with colorful rectangles

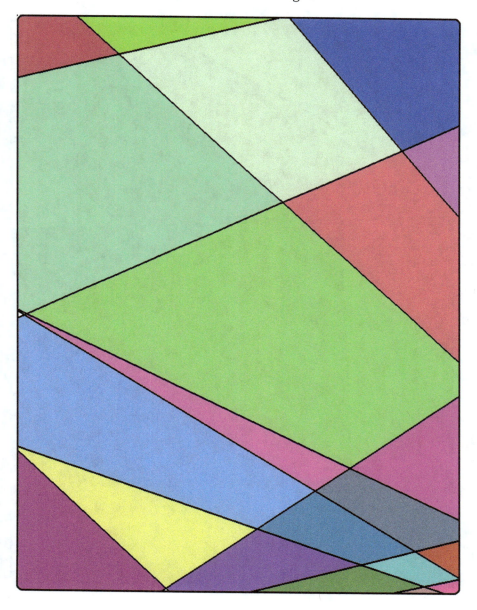

27. Random ornament with colorful rectangles

28. Random ornament with colorful rectangles

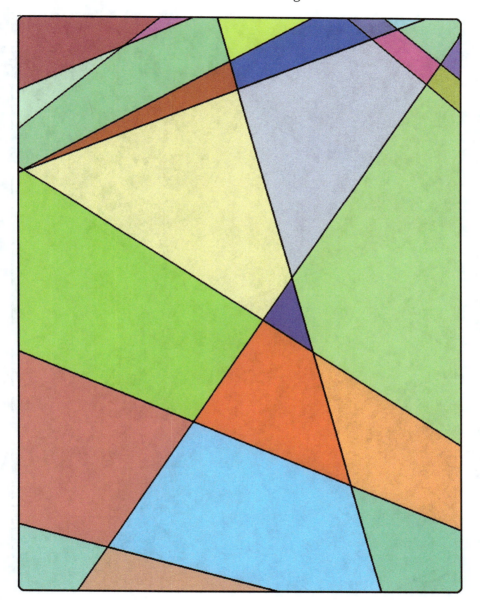

29. Random ornament with colorful rectangles

30. Random ornament with colorful rectangles

31. Random ornament with colorful rectangles

32. Random ornament with colorful rectangles

33. Random ornament with colorful rectangles

34. Random ornament with colorful rectangles

35. Random ornament with colorful rectangles

36. Random ornament with colorful rectangles

37. Random ornament with colorful rectangles

38. Random ornament with uppercase letters

39. Random ornament with uppercase letters

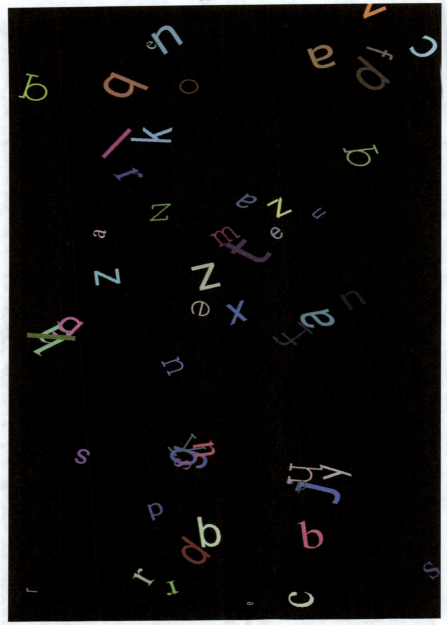

40. Random ornament with uppercase and lowercase letters

41. Random ornament with uppercase, lowercase letters and symbols

42. Random ornament with numbers

43. Random ornament with letters, symbols and numbers

As we reach the final strokes of this book, consider this not an end but a beginning. Your journey in the world of Digital Random Art is just starting, filled with infinite possibilities.